Then & Now

Then & Now

poems

James Cummins

Swallow Press / *Ohio University Press* // Athens

Swallow Press / Ohio University Press, Athens, Ohio 45701
© 2004 by James Cummins
Printed in the United States of America
Swallow Press / Ohio University Press books are printed on acid-free paper ∞ ™

12 11 10 09 08 07 06 05 04   5 4 3 2 1

Acknowledgments
Grateful acknowledgment is made to the editors of the journals in which some
of the poems in this book first appeared: *Antioch Review* ("Collegiality," "Echo");
Euphony ("Orpheus Fixes Himself a Cup of Tea"); *Flights* ("The Clockmaker,"
"Poster Children"); *Gulf Coast* ("Poetry Reading"); *The Mississippi Review* ("Against
Wordplay," "Doing Lunch," "For Margaret"); *The Paris Review* ("Edmund Wilson
and His Wife, Elena, Have Dinner with Edna St. Vincent Millay and Her Husband,
Eugen Boissevain, August 6, 1948," "From a Notebook," "To Helen Vendler and
Jorie Graham at Harvard," "We'll Always Have Paris"); *Southern Indiana Review*
("Prayer for My Daughters"); *Western Humanities Review* ("Now and Then,"
"Practical Immortalities").

"Echo" also appeared in *Best American Poetry 1998*, edited by John Hollander and
David Lehman.

"Edmund Wilson and His Wife, Elena, Have Dinner with Edna St. Vincent
Millay and Her Husband, Eugen Boissevain, August 6, 1948" was reprinted in
Harper's Magazine, June 2001.

I would like to thank David Schloss and David Sanders for their generous help in
preparing this manuscript.

Library of Congress Cataloging-in-Publication Data
Cummins, James.
   Then & now : poems / by James Cummins.
      p. cm.
   ISBN 0-8040-1066-8 (cloth : acid-free paper) — ISBN 0-8040-1067-6
(pbk. : acid-free paper)
   I. Title: Then and now. II. Title.
PS3553.U455 T48 2004
811'.54—dc22

                        2003023922

For Margaret, my joy

Contents

I

II

I

Spoken Nervously by Torchlight to Angry Villagers

Look, if there should be
life after death, I'll merely
be guilty of foolishness;

and if the sign of salvation
is truly a new car or house,
then I'm only to be pitied

in death as I was in life;
but if there should turn out to be
the phenomenon of *grace*,

different from the almost
unbearable beauty of the world,
and if it consists of God

letting me know for a brief
moment I'm not alone—
by putting a huge arm, say,

around my shoulders, or giving
a thumbs-up sign across
an amazingly if not

improbably large room—
all I can claim, as they angle
a needle in a vein and load me

into the van, is it's surely
the least of my problems
that I didn't believe.

The buildings stand, with all *intention* changed
from what designed and built them. Killer ants,
their Gallic genes resembling old blueprints,
by chance achieved a neoclassic age.

But building such a world's beyond them now.
They name their power that of *unmaking*—
authors of destabilizing force. (Marking
one's time is a kind of genius: *Tao*, Dow.)

The French can lie, and yet again can lie;
they lie standing or sitting, if so required.
And no penalty for their lies—their true, tired
allies must now bear their *discourse*. Or try.

The bully comes when you are most vain—
Time's answer to your flourishing. The Doubt
that follows almost father to that gout.
But to ally oneself with time and change,

instead of to resist, is mask, *regent*—
a flattery of time, betraying real
discourse . . . You bend, seasoning the eel,
pretending to yourself you are its agent.

Lullaby of Broadway

A stag's head came to me, filling my dream
with beauty. I drew back from it in wonder,
saw its great shoulders, the muscles of its flank.
Then I seemed to sleep again, and wake—
and the stag's head, torn from its body, lay
beside the stream, bleeding into the water . . .
My eyes cloud over as I watch the ships
the white men anchor off our shallow coast.
They bring ashore objects as numberless
as stars. I look down at what I carry:
it's useful, clean. My heart's a burden, joy:
it tries to understand what awful fear
is loose upon the land that a stag's head—
torn from its body, sent in smoke of dreams—
must take this form in sleep to speak to me.
These new men took from us the small island
between the two great rivers and the sea.
The young will stare at these beads I bring back.
I had no choice: the spirit moved through me
to give away our land to men I fear.
I watched their eyes, their hands, and never saw
compassion or forbearance or remorse.
For them desire is measured by numbers—
their eyes would make me nothing, unname me;
they'll take the rest from us when more ships come.
I simply bought us time, a dream I thought
no man could measure out. But I was wrong.
The young are strong, brave men. They followed me
in battle without fear; they heard my voice.

They have not looked into the eyes like beads.
I salvaged from the enemy these beads,
the symbol of his hate: it will be years
before the mirror will give back the face
of what he lost. Then he will choke on beads.
The memory of beads. Numberless beads.

Spring Comes to Hamilton Avenue

In spring the pear trees blossom
on Hamilton Avenue
and for a week or two
the young black kids with nowhere to go
sell their dope to each other
under resplendence.

For a week or two
the Blue Jay is a bright eye
and the old beaks who gather there
to sort neighborhood gossip
remember their own.

Ray is gone now, the self-proclaimed
"Mayor of Northside,"
but there are several Rays left
warming on benches
under the white and blowing trees;

and this morning, across the street,
Bill steps out from the clutter
of his hardware store,
tilts a red cup to his lips,
then smiles around
with a general benignity
under the white flowers.

So much pain in the world—
so brilliant its occasional release!
A bus moves by slowly,

an old woman at a wedding;
a girl stands up on her bike—

how I loathe the ones
who say we've fallen
from some glory;
how I loathe their god.

From a Notebook

1. The Frame

We offer each other a dark
brew. But we must drink.

A seduction is the setting up
of parameters. The frame.

We offer the hole inside
that must be filled,

but get no takers. So we make
believe:

the surface changes,
human by human,

but what's beneath remains
the mouth of hell.

2. Big Pot

I live in a hell not entirely
of my own devising. God,
what children my parents
were, are. The blood-
curdling look of my father,

in that photograph after
we've come back to
Cincinnati: even he is
a child, if a murderous
one. A murderous rage

at *her* informs him. No,
not my mother. His.
We make symbols in
language like the word
"loves," and think

because she never said
she "loves" him, he
rebels, sobers up, attempts
maturity, loses, grows
increasingly bitter, then

lunatic with fury, twisting
the flesh under his
daughter's arms, to leave
bruises, *wanting*
to leave bruises . . . Then,

he sobers up again,
from that long drunk,
but not from the glimmer
the "ponies" gave him,
that he never realized—

or did he?—wasn't
money and a future,
but a present look

into the lost heart's
land: when the horses

ran, something quickened
in him, different from
what thrilled to the flick
of cards, or ring of coins—
or later, the much

more satisfying click,
on felt, of plastic
chips. And sometimes,
the rattle of them, when
there were so many.

3. The Comedian

Narcissism is an occupational
hazard for poets. Seriously,
you can't do this stuff
night after night, and survive.

You have to take breaks,
vacations. Nothing wrong
with vacations, sleeping
late. T. S. Eliot said

you had to lie around
on a couch for long periods.
You can imagine him lying
around on a couch,

in his suit, of course,
the high stiff collar,
hair slicked back
with some kind of gel—

what did they call it
in those days? Maybe
you can see him in silk,
an elegant dressing jacket,

but the hair still slicked
back. The way some people
envision Sherlock Holmes—
reclining, ratiocinating.

I am truly, deeply crazy,
and some nights I am granted
the ability to see how much,
for a little while. This alone

should convince me there's
a God, but it doesn't.
I don't need God, our kind
of poet says, but he thinks

he means this as a positive.
What about the negative,
when you find yourself with
yourself, in a small room,

in the long run? Sherlock Holmes
is the only thinking allowed
men in our climes and times:
the rest is genius, and who

understands that? Unless
you're a poet, and you do:
the grandest narcissism
is genius, and the others

suspect you might be right.
So much depends, not on
a wheelbarrow, but that
Einstein was a nice guy.

4. By Half

"I'm a fraud," he wrote easily, feeling feelings
of fraudulence the French feel, when he wrote
that. He groaned. Even his feelings of fraudulence
were fraudulent, even the language that described
seemed to be uttered by a fraudulent voice.
Of course we project our feelings onto reality,

but sometimes it's the reverse, and reality
projects its feelings onto us. And those feelings
are real: you are worthless as a voice—
your thinking, acting, feeling merely a rote
recitation, the language you select to describe
your commitment, by describing its fraudulence,

a lesson in, and avoidance of, real fraudulence.
At this point you should forget about reality.
Live in your head awhile, let yourself describe
completed circles, arabesques—forms of feelings
the philosophers discovered so long ago, and wrote
such hymns of praise to in their "authentic" voices.

5. Denouement

You've always failed, and sought that denouement.
The more you haven't done what you need to,
the less is left for you to do. The need
remains, a wound in your side like Christ's wound.

No Christian, you are startled by that image.
Maybe all "He" was was Being splayed
upon the board, or couch, of any god.
Remember, he asked who did this to him.

A father's anger shows you doubt, despair.
The face of Christ turned toward empty heaven.
It scares you; you must cover up your face,
when you look into that, alone. The man

who turns back can love man or woman,
he so longs to be pierced by a sweet face.
Was that what caused the sad rage of his father:
he learned to be a woman from his mother?

6. Monster

If only there was no one that I fail—
a common dream of men: to be alone
at least is to be free; that's what they think.
But that freedom is just another jail:
there, no one buffers you from being you.
The monster that they say you are, you are.

Poster Children

My right side staring fixedly,
the left a blend of sneer and cry:
the Academy is where I live.
Not that the Sturms and Drangs
ever pick me first at recess,
but neither do they pick me last.

I'm pictured next to a soft man
of sensibility, his soft face
half in soft shadow, his left
eye in concert with his raised
lip: he'll make you love him,
damn it, love his receding hair.

We're both down from a man
who's left Barbados for the Big
Apple. He wears a native skull
cap of some sort, colorful
against a background black
as the cosmos he comes out of,

toward us: what do we *really*
know about him? And, of course,
far to the left of us all, Henry—
Berryman, cigarette at right
angle to his neck, the shaft
of a direct hit. Such allowance

we make for the lunatic
and poet. The rest in various

versions of themselves: this
one demonic, that one just
a regular Jo, if irregularly so.
I tape us to the office door.

To Helen Vendler and Jorie Graham at Harvard

1.

I love the way the self-appointed save us.
I love how love enables all those good-
not-great minds to decide we don't get it.
The seeing of the not-there in the there
is virtue in a poet, less so in love:
love fails to see anointing is itself
a fallacy about creation, death . . .
We wonder at love's righteousness, its cheek.

The finger pointing at the moon is not,
I've heard, the moon. What does anointing teach,
but the anointer's hope? (And were there oils
involved? A powerful vibration, hum?)
We know this need is self-love in disguise—
will no one rid us of anointers, then?

2.

The wrong new ones won out at century's start:
the Woolfs were at the door, Carlos, Old Ez.
Felicities of self instead of phrase
would be the new measure, the new lockstep,
replacing Vanity with vanities.
It took a while, enforcement of the new—
these democrats, these haters of the Jew.
A nod to Stevens, and the field was theirs.

The poem on the page is still a mirror—
gives back the one who made it, in its frame;
gives back the one who reads in it a truth
beyond his ken. Or hers. Now self is all:
thus we become the darkness that we love
to talk about, claim we're the product of.

Tails

The sperm knows
he is nothing, the egg
everything, in

place. The gained
goal means only
he is not spill

upon the barren
ground, womb,
but living on

in higher form. Here
anxiety begins:
no meaning in

oneself, none
possible in reached
exalted other.

Men give up
slowly, lover
by lover.

"No ideas but in things" is an idea,
after all, and not simply that a thing
is better than its idea. *No world
but mine* is what that ploy suggests: the self
as banner of some god. The worn-out face
of your god now must bow down to my god.

In our beginning, Jews invented God.
He broke bread, laughed with them, a new idea
about the human world. And this god's face
was mild yet stern, insisting on one thing:
"God" is just the way we hear the self—
our first allegiance must be to *this* world.

That brilliant trope was lost upon the world,
which then made sure the Jews devised a god
of war, a callow god, with which the self
identified, became the false idea
of power over things. The privileged *thing*
replaced the glory of the human face.

To be a Christian *is* to wear "God's face"—
a nightmare god of greed, who knows the world
belongs to him by right. The measured thing
behind the mask—the red hole crying "God"
and pillage camouflaged as Idea—
abstracts us all in service to "Himself."

The other spawn, Islam, deludes itself
a man is strong to loathe a woman's face.

Its vain men robe themselves in the idea
they are powerful and make the world
veil itself, too, before their righteous god.
Two "faiths," revealing no idea, thing,

but hatred, arrogance: ideas, things.
Eliot thought abstraction frayed the self
into false premises, one of them "God."
Before Plato, man's face was still a face,
not a marker played out to trick the world.
Now love is marketed, mere idea

that faces down opposed ideas of self.
Men blow up things built to a different god,
displace death onto Christ, Allah, the world.

Scene at the End of the World

The you-know-what will hit the you-know-what,
you know. Sometimes, a sense of set design—
of what they want behind them as they whine
about the years of stored-up rage and hurt—
diverts them from the fences they would mend;
and suddenly red tooth and claw are out.
The lion roars against the Rock of Doubt;
the lioness strikes home—the roar and rend
played out almost as if by someone else.
One tells himself he's honoring the new;
the other fears this makes her past untrue:
not to be known is not to know oneself.
The backdrop is their lonely castle's keep;
they rip and claw. The children are asleep.

Home Fires

Is there a paradigm some wives invent,
of husband marked with tail and cloven hoof?
His neediness is all she needs for proof:
he "needs" no more than what she will dispense.
Yet she's indignant at imagined slights.
He's "not-quite-human," as she takes his measure—
and not-quite-human, either, is his pleasure—
though she is "only" human, by her lights.
By his lights they both lied those years ago,
for reasons of their own; and now the lie
becomes the living truth. *If love is why
he leaves, why did he stay?* A double blow
to what she tries to hold onto: her head,
hurting and spinning in the marriage bed.

Collegiality

A man takes off his glasses, after a hard day
at work, squeezes his nose, and rubs his eyes
so hard he scoops out an eyeball by mistake.
He cups it gently, still attached to his face,
goes out to the car, realizes he can't do it,
calls 911. At the hospital, they prep his head.

His eyeball floats in a dish next to his head.
What the hell have I done? "What a day!"
he jokes with the orderlies. "Never forget it!"
They don't respond. Tears fill up his eyes.
Oh, god, I can't cry! He wants to wipe his face,
but he's afraid. *Dear God, make it a mistake,*

he prays, *please make it all a sad mistake . . .*
Then he's out, and they start in on his head.
"I don't even look," says one, "at the face.
If I thought about it, it would ruin my day!"
Another nods. Above his mask, his eyes
signal agreement. "Why I continue to do it,

I haven't the foggiest! Each day I feel it:
the constant ritual address of mistake."
"Yes! *Yes!*" exclaims a third. Her eyes,
too, were sending signals from her head.
"Oh, it's so *true*—every day! Every *day!*
Oh, God, I feel it, too—face after face

of derision, carelessness, panic—my face
begins to mirror theirs—oh, yes, I *feel* it!"

The others stare at her. "It's quite a day,"
the first one resumes, watchful. "No mistake
about that." The second one nods his head.
The third one blushes, dropping her eyes.

Suddenly, as if the eyeball had eyes,
it squirts between them, slips off the face,
distending floorward from that sad head,
until a soft sucking "pop" severs it.
The garrulous one then makes a mistake
she'll live with the rest of her days—

more than a mistake: she steps on it. *Her* face
distends, eyes popping out of *her* head—
the others call her "Big Foot" to this day.

Orpheus Picks Up His Dry Cleaning

"Walking cliché" is what your friend calls me—
two kids, one wife, a house, a job, some *angst*.
Maybe she's right. I don't protest against
the obvious, what everybody sees—
or would see, if I had the guts to out
myself, declare my life has changed, confess.
It's not the only source of my distress,
this fragile life, that I have come to doubt.
What can love do, effect? What can love be?
Do I deserve its benefit, its debt?
Each minute is a thought of you, a net
of absences, and sweet contingencies.
My love, you doubt yourself, not me, or love;
oh, the delight, and weariness, of love . . .

Weary Orpheus

Oh, the delight and weariness of love
will have their several meanings. My friend
believes you will betray me, in the end.
I tell her that she fails to measure love
from inside out, but I'm afraid. You please
yourself with other men; you need their eyes,
the self-esteem this acquiescence buys.
Love is illness, the saying goes: dis-ease.
Oh, I am sick with love, and sick of love—
the minute-by-minute waiting, the death
these minutes calibrate, each conscious breath—
the nights without you, I am speaking of.

Orpheus Watches His Daughter Blow Out Candles

Divorce means walking out of many lives,
not just the one. The single flames go out
like candles on a cake, and only doubt,
not wishes, climbs the air. But love connives
to have its cake and eat it, too. Or so
some claim—they say love's just a piece of cake.
Run that one by the lovers, whose worlds shake
at each phone call, each misread look. We show
them their nerve fails—they can't take that. And ours?
We haven't any nerve, just nerves. We rue
this feeling that love makes the past untrue;
we aren't gloating as we steal the hours.
All lovers understand betrayal well:
it's love itself that leads them up from hell.

Orpheus Fixes Himself a Cup of Tea

It's not so wise to fall asleep too early;
nerve and bone, muscle and tendon, knit
in sleep; the clock of ligament is set
to wake us when the nourishment is barely
at the full: when limb and eye and brain
have walked and drunk and sung their fill below
the moon within; and, sated, rise to go,
as lovers rise to go before the dawn.
It's not so wise to lie awake alone,
before the light; it's not so wise to hear
the one or two sounds that the night can bear
to make, the sound of life becoming stone,
or vanishing. The story's lived in dream;
and if it wake too soon, is lived again.

Tattoo

We have *moment*, but also *duration;*
we must define so we can re-define.
We make our mark upon another's thought
to hear ourselves, in order to be heard.

Love names an emptiness gone unnamed;
the lover burns to tell his lover truth;
and she in turn desires to be told.
Desires this of another lover, too.

Echo

Lovers check each other—"How are you?"—
when love is going, but before it's gone.
"Oh, I'm better. The nausea's settled down.
The mad howling stopped the other night."
Some rueful laughter on the other end.
"Me, too," she whispers, in her quiet voice,

"me, too." He thinks: I love her quiet voice.
"Yesterday, at the market, I saw you—"
she catches, laughs. It's hard for love to end.
It's hard to wake up, certain that it's gone.
He says, "I thought about you all last night,
but I'm better. The nausea's settled down."

They never say that love has settled down,
that it no longer uses its sweet voice
to carry them in boats across the night.
If you deny love, love will deny you;
the nighttime of its daytime voice is gone,
as you will be. It's hard for love to end.

But any love is difficult to end—
all endings seem to whisper, then lie down,
an old man dying by the fire, soon gone,
as if he'd never lived. Her quiet voice,
that only yesterday spoke just to you,
will soon become a whisper in the night,

then disappear forever from the night.
And there's no preparation for that end.

She laughs again. "I want to be with you."
He understands. He puts the phone back down.
How will he live without her quiet voice?
What will he do, when she's finally gone?

Within a week the moving van is gone.
He works all day and dreads the quiet night.
The day will come when he'll forget her voice;
he has no need or longing for that end.
He'd settle now for keeping dinner down.
He hears again: "*I want to be with you.*"

He stares into the pool of night, her voice
behind him, gone. He monitors the end:
he lies down, hears the faint refrain: "*with you . . .* "

Elegy

So many things we want to ask the dead,
when only yesterday they were alive—
the not-quite-dead, still among us,
still importuning that one last lunch
or phone call we were too busy to give.

But it's not our multifaceted multitasking
selves that keep us from the almost-gone.
It's this glimmer they get, this volubility,
this light that starts to shine out from their heads,
beacon of knowledge not quite grasped,

that makes their faces look suddenly gray,
yet capable of delight and laughter.
Maybe they'll laugh at us, we think,
if we go to lunch with them, or talk.
Maybe they'll drill some pointed observation

or pithy admonition into our heads, phrasings
set in stone by shock the next morning,
when news we knew was coming terrifies
and saddens in our self-regarding woe.
We know quite well the scam they run:

they want to live on in our heads as well
as those they've captured with their voice
already: children, spouses, a household pet,
for heaven's sake, a lowly dog with fleas,
who wonders where to drop the slippers now,

and who'll continue in this stark confusion
until arthritic legs refuse to squat and shit
or amble toward the food. They want
their immortality, the smiling near-dead do:
they want to pass themselves along to you.

Donut Life

Busy, full—even, on occasion, sweet—
with a hole in the middle of it.

Recipes for remedy: Boston
cream pie; cupcakes (white, iced); Cocoa
Krispies; brownies; nonfat cake (once);
Oreos; spoonfuls of whipped cream,
peanut butter, chips; Double-Goo
Butter Cake (local specialty); chocolate-
chip cookies, milk chocolate chunks,
cooking chocolate; strawberries and
cream (health kick); Strawberries
'n Cream Homemade Brand Deluxe
Ice Cream; yogurt; M&M's . . .

Why hadn't they run from each other
as from a terror of death
those many years ago?
She could have had her large house
in Hyde Park, not been "ashamed";
he could have kept his weight down.

(Answer: the sweetness that you know . . .)

The hole frames the sea, black, beyond;
or the cosmos, equally a sea.

Midnight reading, hunched over, lair:
Nietzsche, *Krazy Kat*, *The Baseball
Encyclopedia*, Library of America editions

of everyone, ZAP, Henderson the Rain
King, actuarial tables, The New
Yorker, -Republic, -Criterion, -York Review
of Books . . . Newsweek.

(Dipping cookies in milk . . .)

Busy, full, even on occasion sweet
life.

II

Solstice Moon

Clouds slip over you rapidly
like silk before desire;
you want the wind to uncover
the high cold circle of you.

I shiver as another year
falls from me like a gown.
I lift my arms like a lover
to you, like a child.

Practical Immortalities

A poem is a moment in a life
that stands for many moments, and goes on
in time, a partner in a dance, in love;
it doesn't conquer time, but slows it down,
so other moments can be lived in full.

How can we not want this? How can we not
employ it in our battles with our deaths?
My western life had so much east in it;
the eastern one had so much of my death.
It was the west that arced me toward my birth.

You have to be hard on yourself—and too,
you must forgive. You can't do only one.
The first will tell you where your lie begins;
the second, where it ends; and you go on.
You have to know your lie, and go beyond.

The minds who mind you can't do this. They can't
forgive, because they can't forgive themselves.
The ones who do it every day just nod:
you quicken toward the world, it quickens back.
But that which can't contain you, shuts you out.

You have a day, and then you have one more.
That's all there is. And it's enough. You spend
the morning underneath the falls; at noon,
you eat. You stretch it out. You stretch it out,
and when the evening comes, prepare to sleep.

Now and Then

Of course the middlebrow in any age
strike to the heart of earth, pretending joy
in juices they find there. Willing the heart
becomes, in time, believed in as the way.
The wilder ones, beards streaked, enjoin the rest
to Bacchanalian revel, wallet-sized.
The cyclical is the historical—
without the doubt, and paid for with a card.
The other way, there's so much more to lose;
the moon reveals her cold carnality;
a breeze might be a hand. The sex that shakes
another's frame, and leaves it void, can mate
with every death within you, and require
you leave upon the earth no single touch.

2

Just six weeks married when they had it out:
I will not take your mother's place, he said,
and be the nurse I was brought up to be
by mine . . . She wheezed, working the asthma game:
Take care of me, I'm sick, give me that warmth—
the only way she lured her mother's love.
She's lost in time, he thought, and held her close;
and watched his life flash forward in despair.
The charge, the stone, was his. By whose account?
What did he love in her? In sex, she drew

away from him, as if he weren't big
enough to fill her need. She thought her mouth,
and distance, would suffice; she punished him—
the father now, who beat her, then would cry.

3

Outwardly, they were happy; they had pride.
The scorn she showed when he begged to be close
helped him in other ways; she taught him how
to dress, and be reserved, and order food.
And please the older ones up the food chains
he must ascend, though he was quick to learn:
he ate. He was a swallower, of course,
by trade: he drank and swallowed with a smile.
And she had what she wanted. Or at least,
what she could see: she wouldn't die, not now.
Transition from the mother to the man
complete, she hadn't lost a thing: her beauty
conquered all. When he got mad, she cried
and promised change. Next morning, she forgot.

4

Lest we forget, we men were needed once.
Maybe the stories told around the fire
relieved, foremost, our own anxieties;
but you could nurse a child in peace and warmth,
and share the food. We loved to share the food;
we loved to share whatever we had killed.
To take life from that death was not unlike
what you put in those eager mouths each day.

A faith is never much, yet everything.
Without one, you career off through the dark.
That was the nature of the hunt: a faith.
A gift to still the lunacy of men.
We couldn't call you "first cause," though you were:
how could you feel what it feels like to win?

5

They killed their child—oh, all legal, of course:
Roe v. Wade, "taking control"—panic,
really. They lived some weeks on just green beans,
peanut butter—how could *they* have a child?
There would be time. The doctor told the students
gathered round: "Here's the healthiest vulva
you'll ever see." Boy, girl—they never knew.
Afterward, dulled out, she marked the wrong boxes
on forms; they had to pay some ninety bucks
they didn't have. The tension broke; he cursed;
she turned her face away, beaten. He saw
what he had done, but couldn't take it back.
The lines were drawn; she had her full excuse:
he was a beast. The deepest guilt is shared.

6

He did things in the world to prove he could;
he stoked the office politics to see
who would act out; he counseled wounded souls
who loved him for his listening and concern.
He tried to give, tried to defend himself:
he learned to cut expenditures of time.

He wrecked the marriage of a friend from pride,
not lust; he never touched the wife. (He made
lists of regrets, and put her name on top.)
He blundered through his life all day, then brought
home reassuring words and hands to her.
She calmed down, lying next to him; some nights,
he calmed down, too, and felt her lonely heart.
They slept the sleep of illness, and waited.

7

Finally, it dawns: you're just not smart enough.
But everyone knows this, who's smart enough—
what you all share with those who think they are
is willingness to let them think they are.
There's rhyme to this: you see the ends of roads
down which they wend in brashness and travail;
you see the badges they accrue, the signs.
But smartness isn't matter; it is time,
the only immortality we've got.
It's just a little door, a little gate,
through which you step; and lifetimes you have tried
to shape dissolve; or better, blend to one—
the one you're living with the other ones,
those smart enough, like you, to know they're dumb.

8

They went to bad movies—Newman, Redford,
two jackanapes with guns. When cleverness
caused grim-faced men to follow them in clouds
of swirling dust, the two cute leads would shrug:

"Who *are* those guys?" It was a joke. Of course,
"they" were their deaths—a catalyst, a scene
against which narcissism could play out
its bloody end. Cornered, wounded—at last,
alarmed—hubris drew them into the sun
for one last dance. But while they'd huddled, coughed,
the twenty men had grown to five thousand;
five thousand gun blasts altered their design.
Back home, he chuckled to himself. She asked
him *What?* He couldn't put it into words.

9

Then illness struck; four years of terror, pain,
for both; she almost died two nights. He knelt
beside her, willing breath into lungs flat
as hope, too far away to risk the phone,
seconds too short. His anger mixed with fear;
he kissed her hand, and cried, and kissed her hand.
For hours all he did was kiss her hand,
and whisper to her it would be all right.
Finally, the medics came, hung up IV's,
gave her a breathing treatment and a shot.
He was irrelevant; he got her clothes—
shampoo, toothbrush—and followed in the car.
Hospital lights made her look small and young;
and in her eyes, belief he wouldn't fail.

10

Never to know another, or be known—
now that's the saddest story, isn't it?

The one our century told us with such glee.
"We can't be sure it's particle or wave"—
"The instrument makes measurement unclear"—
those fustian voices, fussing with themselves—
"All meaning is suspect, except my meaning"—
then home, and knock the kids around, or worse.
You think you know it all, it's clear you don't;
the "Other-wholly-other" is the proof
we are the same, if only for a while.
And time's the point: the eye love passes through.
Good metaphor is not approximate;
neither is love. Though love does change, in time.

Prayer for My Daughters

I love them too much to love myself enough;
no, don't put it on them, even though
to see those faces dim, to see fear
of the world in their eyes will darken mine.
Maybe at that moment my smile, the way
I try to look right into their eyes
with my love, will give them strength, speak
to them the way a father can't in life.
But maybe the way I look into their eyes
will haunt them forever with my inadequacy—
who is ever adequate to his child?
Oh I can see how a father's fear
might keep them with him forever, steal
a natural desire to leave and make
some beautiful thing, to bring back:
give me the strength to go with them
a little way past the door of the house;
let them forget me gradually, though I
remain with them awhile. One morning,
I won't be there, is all; they'll see
if I'm to live on they must keep me
alive in their minds. Let something
of me live on in them, let them be proud
of this, though I am not worthy.

After These Messages

"Never having said you're sorry,
now you must say good-bye.
The pain in your stomach has spread
to your side, to your back.

'Honey, it's your turn,'
you whisper, in the hospice glow
of these last days together.
'You'll do a better job. I know.'

And damn it, you do know—
how she'll run a tight ship at first,
and when she gets past the fear,
how she'll loosen up, enjoy life.

Okay, so she may never enjoy life,
but she will loosen up.
And you won't be there to see:
bearing the weight of her

outwaiting you was death.
What terrible wrong did you
do her, that she remembers
with such implacable love?

No matter. What counts now
is that you can rest easy
with your morphine pump.
Metro Life. We care."

2

"'The ignorant are in the field, in numbers.'
Sounds like a message telegraphed
back to headquarters, doesn't it?
But the ignorant are versions of ourselves,
and therefore only dangerous in love.
The truly stupid, though, are frightening:
tea bag brains never steeped enough
in words and touch and smell to see
the light in someone else's brain
shoot out at the eye. Instead,
the uncompleted self projects its lack
of self-regard on faces it can't see,
and hears instead of screams the roar
its own inchoate, bleak becoming makes.
It doesn't want love; it wants money—
money not metaphor, but translation.
You are the metaphor: you're in
the way. National Security Systems.
Don't leave a light on for them."

3

"You don't want to claim
for yourself great honesty,
courage, or over-the-top
sexual prowess:

the gunslingers of the opposition
are always hankering, itchy-
fingered, in the next town.
Better to be designate—

thought of instead of thinking—
though the ones who name
usually are too busy naming
themselves or friends:

a kindness toward them
comes back tenfold
in silence. But isn't silence
what you need? No road

exists you can be set
upon but what you do
the setting. Better
to remember a day

long ago when desire
was distant, when what
came to hand sufficed.
Let what comes to hand

suffice: leather, a V-6 that
eats your friends for lunch.
The Inamorata 666i.
Let the world call you names."

4

"'You come in alone, you go out alone.'
That's what the fathers tell you.
At least my father did.

And all the men I've known like me
had fathers like him
who told them the same thing.

Often in life I've tried
to think of an image that described
this anxiety of my father.

An even, flowing river of death
is not always what he stared into,
but was always the sound he heard

behind everything he did.
Now you've come
to that level of exhaustion

that is like an underground river,
approached through trees and soil
black as the black rocks

along that river, and as wet:
no suns blaze here
to make the rocks less wet.

Grove Spring Cemetery
and Funeral Centre.
Be sure."

Doing Lunch

You have lunch with a friend.
You put on a false face for him,
because he is your friend.
You want to spare him your maunderings,
your lies and malfeasance.

But this is just what your friend desires,
because he is your friend.
He wants your face to fall open
in front of him and twitch
like a rabbit hit on the fly.

He says he wants the latest word
from the border region between
narcissism and an inner life. And laughs.
Shamelessly, you tell him everything,
because he is your friend.

Bay Bus Terminal, San Francisco, 1974

In a dream I saw a woman I worked with,
taking want ads over the telephone—
tent-like Bedouin clothing, gold hoop rings
in ears that heard no good word about men;
hot moist eyes a smear under her brow,
daring you to give them a good reason.
I couldn't fathom why she hated me,
until the day I quit. Her protégé—
Karyn, eighteen—declared her love for me.
Surprised me at the Bay Bus terminal,
gave me a card with childlike note and scrawl,
then kissed me with the passion of a child—
artless, confused, but whole and giving, true.
I held her, though I didn't understand;
and then I understood: she came, shuddering
against me, and I held her minutes more.
I looked across the terminal: no one
had noticed, cared. I looked at her, her eyes
amazed with tears of grief and joy. Alarmed,
I tried to do the right, good thing; then too,
I was aroused—should she know that or not?
Should I enclose my own desire in hers,
as she said she wanted? Or did good-bye
just take this form—projection of a self
on someone safe, who understands the hope?
She touched me then; I didn't back away;
she understood. I still feel her shy hand.
My bus was filling up; I had to leave.
I brushed her cheek and felt what lovers feel:

lovers' tears, wetting the palm. I rode
across the Bay Bridge, through Oakland, let
my hand stay open, cold instead of wet.

Epithalamium for a Teacher

He likes the younger ones, he likes the hurt
ones, ones whose eyes show back to him his need.
They grasp instinctively how much to flirt—
how much damage to show—to make him heed.
His new wife's fears will finally abate,
as more and more old lovers graduate.

Old Man

I carry my debt with me, on my back.
Those TV cop shows seem to say it best:
you come from nowhere, you don't know jack.

My family was like a hunting pack—
a ring of faces more like wounds not dressed.
I carry my debt with me, on my back.

You take with you precisely what you lack—
a paradox by which the poor are blessed.
You come from nowhere? You don't know jack.

Not that you haven't met that asshole, Jack.
He comes around, an uninvited guest.
You carry *his* debt with you, on your back.

Jack's angrier than you, and that's a fact.
Who knows the burdens we have all repressed?
You come from nowhere, you don't know jack.

I'm out of smokes. I have to get a pack.
I can't remember when I've touched a breast.
I carry my debt with me, on my back.
I came from nowhere. I don't know jack.

Nurses

My mother sees the gravestones in her head:
Mary, Skelly, Katie. Her recent dead.

It puts all that has gone before in doubt.
She knows she'll take her place with them, and soon.

Arm in arm, we watch a hunter's moon.
She's too afraid to let these memories out.

The lawn I walk across with her is steep.
I too have troubles come to me in sleep.

I am her son: I take care of, and care.
Two nurses turning in the evening air.

The Player

Don't ask him what the game is that he plays;
if you don't know, he's got no time for you.
The reason he makes art is that it pays:
it gets him things. And these things get him through.
He networks, panders, swaps a smile or sob;
others in turn trade what they have that gleams:
a summer conference, grants, awards, a job;
with no sense that the tainted prize demeans.
As time goes by, the player feels a draft,
imagining his head upon a platter—
aging, all players fetishize the craft,
to compensate the failing subject matter.
Whatever else the journey is, it's not
the journey in: what art he sells, he bought.

Against Wordplay

The ones who deny
what happened in their childhoods,
the emotions this causes them to feel,
the actions it causes them to take,

choose wordplay.
One can hide in the tall mirrors
of words. Many have pretended
that surfaces are depths,

that the several surfaces of a word
constitute a depth,
not a lexicon of mirrors
in which to hide.

Celan was one
whose inability to feel
caused him almost to explode
when history obliterated his childhood.

(There is no human scale
in death camps,
reason has no rational way
to frame that mirror.)

We think what we get from our parents
can be controverted
by the incontrovertible
reality of how we frame our fear:

we use what we got
to beat what we get
into the ground,
it is a tantrum of pain.

America, we are invisible
in the vast spaces of your money!
You make us to lie down at night
far from each other's death,

the pain of which would burst from our lungs
were we not paid so well
to hide in the tall mirrors
of wordplay.

Doherty Christmas Show

The innocence of a child
is the most powerful rebuke.
All the ways we conspire
to cheat ourselves of life

are knocked for a loop
by her smile or, better,
the *ho-ho-ho* sound
she makes at the Christmas

show, her head turned toward
Eddie, already the class
clown, flipping his tie
up over his ear,

and letting it slide back
down. She takes for
granted boys do this,
at least this boy;

she sees past him,
yet includes him,
as she measures the effect
the group is having,

or just slips into
the beautiful words,
as only the most radiant
can hide in them.

Poetry Reading

Those grim ones unacquainted with humor
lack, too, a sense of the serious:
they know only the gravity of the self,
weighty enough to keep them on the ground.

And when they want to start up, fly—
when they take up jogging, or French—
you can see them congratulating themselves,
as they drift by you, half naked, alone.

Tonight you hear one of them speak
what she says are her innermost thoughts.
She has returned from a month in Paris,
now is writing some poems called "Etudes."

There is longing. There is hope, despair.
We follow her up and down the boulevards,
mittened and mufflered, her white breath
floating above her like a balloon,

a white cloud she matches to her heart:
"You," she is saying—no doubt the familiar,
but surely not us—we shift uneasily
in our chairs—who? a dog? a parent?

Baudelaire?—until, astonished, we realize
she's talking to that little woman in the front
row, who holds her books, smiling—
that little white-crowned woman, her hair

splayed out like a cleaning pad, gentle
and humorless as our speaker, even perhaps her—
what's that?—yes, *muse* has found its place
in the wild vocabulary of those Parisian nights!

And in fact, it *is* she—Herself—so long
invoked, beseeched, by all of us—right here—
her smile not only inspiring but overseeing
the distribution of books for sale!

Edmund Wilson and His Wife, Elena, Have Dinner with Edna St. Vincent Millay and Her Husband, Eugen Boissevain, August 6, 1948

Is it hot in here, or is it just me?
They both seem so much older now than I—
can this be so? Do women age like dogs,
or something out of Wilde? Seven years
for every one we live? He cuts her meat.

Good God, that inward stare! I loved her so.
The self-absorption's thickened like her hide.
I knew all this before, of course. I knew.
And got out early like the pig I am.
She's jowly, tense. *Elderly.* It's nineteen years . . .

What was Elena saying as they left?
Arm in arm, as if I'd ceased to be?
They walked along the garden for an hour,
Elena kindly offering E. her laugh.
Two women, arm in arm, whose toes I've—

What? What'd I say? Blurted something out—
but what? It must have been unpleasant: clouds
are forming on the brow of Mt. Monadnock.
I've added to the burden of his days!
Good Christ, am I going through the change?

Why are they looking at me with such hate?
Why can't I just remember what I said?
We've drunk too much; we always drink too much.

I hear *Herself*—she calls my name loudly,
a tone of bemusement hiding her rage:

"So are you going to pass him the gravy,
or must the three of us go over there,
and by God take the boat by force?" I see
Elena's face, alarmed; I look at Gene,
his face savage, full of remorse; then down

at those gravy-less potatoes. I stare
again at E., at E.—are we *all* insane?
"Of course," I mumble, "the gravy." I look
about wildly—thank God, it's near my plate!
Is there no window in this goddamn house?

Parasite

It is to be a parasite,
to be complete. To be complete—
to be well-fed, lazy, benign—
one lives on others' work, and fear.

To parasites the obvious
is what the world presents, and mulls;
the disconcerted world is dashed,
elated, mystified, by turns;

the world, in short, remains the world.
Only the parasite must die;
so he grows fat, desiring, calm.
The wisdom of the world is balm,

at any moment false, or true.
The parasite, recalcitrant,
reclines, and eats another grape.
The world knows all about him, too.

Dream with Fred Astaire

I smoked a joint with Fred Astaire
once, in a dream. We waited
in a noisy, greasy car repair shop—
though as it happened I reclined
quite elegantly on a *chaise longue*,
and we conversed in French.

Perhaps I should be clear
about the French—I spoke English
as an Englishman might think
a Frenchman would—or as Fred
might pretend to be royalty
in a cheap tux on ship with Ginger,
beaming forth his inanities—
and as I did so I raised a Gallic
eyebrow and handed Fred the joint.

At first he sniffed it, inhaled
the drifting smoke, then broke
it open, found a seed, raised
a Gallic eyebrow back—
and ate the whole. I nodded wisely,
as if Eric Blore or Charlie Ruggles
were working on our cars.

Fred sat on a molded plastic chair,
like someone visiting the sick.

We smoked French and spoke hemp—
I mean, we spoke French and smoked hemp—

while Fred smiled like someone
who knew the tricks but now
was too old to play them.

It seemed like wisdom.

I said—in French, you know—
I said to him, "You haf geeven me
moosh delight, moosh delight,
een life."

He smiled again, this time a bit
resignedly, there was even
a patronizing look as he reached
into his jacket for a pen!

I made a Gallic *moue*, shrug,
lifted a Gallic eyebrow, made
a Gallic opening of hands:
"Autograph? What wood I doo
with thees?" my gestures said.
"I haf my dreams . . . " The joint
had reappeared. We smoked.

Behind us was the sound
of a hammer hitting concrete
in a vast space.

Fred opened his mouth to speak,
but by then I was already waking—
Garbo, this time, in *Grand Hotel*—
and couldn't stay to hear.

Song

The rich aren't lookers,
nor even that smart.
But the rich know one thing:
they're rich and we're not.

All smiles at the party,
all sneers in the lot;
after all, they're rich.
They're rich and we're not.

The rich need our help—
taxes, for a start.
And of course we must love them:
they're rich and we're not.

Old money or new,
laid back or self-start:
the bottom line is
they're rich and we're not.

Needs

A woman I knew
blew into town,
slept with a man who
had a new daughter.
Two nights later,
in a circle of friends,
we passed the tiny body
around in welcome,

as the woman phoned
to tell the father not
again, though she knew
he'd leave first chance,
with some feigned
illness or indignation.

I went to pee.
As I snapped off
the bathroom light,
I heard his wife
bitterly accuse him
in the dark hall.
Then he was gone,
the front door closing
on our averted faces.

It's twenty years,
and their little girl
passes me on the street,
a beautiful woman.

Her father's eyes
look into mine
just for a second,
as if she knew me.

That night I left
before the others,
drove by the motel.
Saw his car displayed
in a floodlit glare,
snow plowed to the edge
of the black lot.
Saw no light on
in any room.

For Margaret

Little Margaret, whose bridges to me I casually blow up;
whose paper airplanes covered with lopsided hearts
         and pictures of yourself and me
I absent-mindedly knock down, thinking of something else,
some grown-up worry: I always believe there will be time
enough. I always think time is a big capacious hat,
a dome beneath which all goodwill will flourish,
a heart we color together on the kitchen table, not
this Daddy-body you come downstairs to be with
after everyone's asleep and you hear my car.
The front door closes softly, but not so softly
you don't feel it, as you slip from your bed to join me.
Do you know I hear the muffled sound of your step
on the stairs with joy? I have no tiredness tonight,
no other thing to think of but the way we drink
each other's body in, each other's joy.

The Clockmaker

First I carve the small wooden figures.
I render lips, buttons, belt, with tiny knives;
then paint them as many colors as will fit.
I'm famous for the eyes: the gray-white
that sets off the luminous blues and browns,
the occasional green. When I finish,
I have four figures, and with these I tell
the story. I might dress a man in boots,
give him an ax; maybe I carve the woman
a butter churn. A boy plays with a dog,
while the daughter—and this is my art—
threads a needle through the eye of a fish.
Slowly, the wheel revolves: Father returns;
Mother looks up, smiling, smoothing her dress;
and the needle slides through that eye . . .
Or I start with a mirrored room. Inside,
a man rehearses lighting cigarettes,
lifting his lighter up from polished glass.
A larger wheel, holding three scenes, turns,
and he smokes elegantly under a chandelier . . .
Later, walking home, a streetlight blooms
behind his double, in shadow, like a dream—
broad lapels and hat brim hide this face,
as it bends forward into a cup of flame . . .
My father played the horses, cards; he timed
the ovals that were spinnings of bright silk.
I carved a clock for him: four men around
a green felt table, the colorful glow
of luck opening its black and red hands.

What mystified my father hardened me
to the wonder of those who buy my clocks,
who assume the irony is lost on me,
walking home at night, though winding streets.

Notes

"Doing Lunch" is for the late Ross Feld.

"Practical Immortalities" is the fifth and concluding part of a longer poem, "The Charles Kuralt Poems."

"Elegy" is for Austin Wright.

"Solstice Moon" is dedicated to Cheryl Wallace.